TOUCHING ROCK

Other AUP Poetry Titles

PERSPECTIVES
George Bruce

THE LOW ROAD HAME
Donald Gordon

INGAITHERINS
Alistair Mackie

WHEN TRUTH IS KNOWN
Ken Morrice

FOR ALL I KNOW
Ken Morrice

A RESURRECTION OF A KIND
Christopher Rush

NOT IN MY OWN LAND
Matthew McDiarmid

TIME GENTLEMEN
Hamish Brown

THE TIMELESS FLOW
Agnes C Carnegie

THE PURE ACCOUNT
poems by Olive Fraser (1909-1977)
collected, selected and introduced by Helena M Shire

POEMS OF THE SCOTTISH HILLS
an anthology
selected by Hamish Brown

SPEAK TO THE HILLS
an anthology of twentieth century British and Irish
mountain poetry
selected by Hamish Brown and Martyn Berry

TOUCHING ROCK

NORMAN KREITMAN

ABERDEEN UNIVERSITY PRESS

First published 1987
Aberdeen University Press
A member of the Pergamon group

© Norman Kreitman 1987

The publisher acknowledges subsidy from the Scottish
Arts Council towards the publication of this volume

British Library Cataloguing in Publication Data

Kreitman, Norman
    Touching Rock: selected poems
    I. Title
    821'.914

    ISBN 0—08—035072—0

PRINTED IN GREAT BRITAIN
THE UNIVERSITY PRESS
ABERDEEN

CONTENTS

Acknowledgements   vii

1 Background in Tuscany   3
   In Torrett, Minorca   4
   Lizard   5
   Lion-tamer   6
   The Lion and the Happy Village   7
   The Yellow Bird and the Poet   8
   Scene with Angler   9
   Going North   10
   North from Penrith   11
   Excluded by Mountains   12
   Stellar Journey   13

2 A Short History of Greek Statuary   17
   Witch Day   18
   The Lineage of Fair Women   19
   Dress Parade   20
   Victorian Sampler   21
   Encounter   22
   Two of You   23
   Bonfire in April   24
   Welcome, Lad   25
   With my Sister   26

3 The Ballad of Gentle John   29
   The Bond   31
   The Homecoming   32
   A Wife Deserted   33
   The Maze   34
   Reflections in a Trojan Pool   35
   Poem in the Mirror   37
   An Error   38
   Monologue with Tulip   39

4 St. Chrystobole   43
   Keeper of the House   44
   October City   45

Hermit   46
Late Rehearsal   47
Therapist   48
White Gladioli   49
It is not Vivaldi   50
Walking Together at Lyne Pool in Winter   51
Question for a Quiet Evening   53

ACKNOWLEDGEMENTS

Acknowledgements are due to the Editors of *Outposts*, *New Poetry*, *Lines Review*, *Chapman*, *Literature and Medicine*, *N. Y.*, and *Akros*, and of the anthologies 'Poems from the Medical World' and 'New Poetry' (Arts Council) Nos. 6 and 8 in which several of these poems first appeared.

1

BACKGROUND IN TUSCANY

What matters is the picture.
So it was that morning in summer
when we sped past the chromium cafes
set in Quattrocento facades, and billowing dust
on the panicky guineafowl, took the higher road from the village.

Under the pencil cypresses
it zigzagged up to the very skyline,
toppled over, and there — in the fold
of a giant's arms, his shoulders high
over elbows of rock — waited the valley we had always anticipated.

Within that green arena
every foreground was the site
for a lilied Annunciation, a trio of saints
raising bony forefingers, or a process of kings,
the location still acting in its culminating drama.

Beyond these stations
in the acres of the backcloth
a solo tree was painted high on a mound,
the labourers stooped in the receding fields
while an arrowhead of birds soared at a distant, stippled hedge.

The horizon was our place too
as heedlessly we moved by routes
that were cracks in the giant's land,
fussing with maps and the heat, unaware
how our way of travelling makes us so vanishingly small.

IN TORRETT, MINORCA

A thin priest, emphatic in black,
stands like an exclamation mark
against a page of limewashed wall.
I walk past with head averted
and wonder, briefly, what he is for.

More engaging is how the hibiscus lifts
a brilliant branch over the hedge
confirming red as the colour of trumpets,
or that elegant girl boasting her figure
as though she had won it in a contest.

And everywhere the sun is bestowing
the old understanding, so that each trellis,
every warmed and crooked flowerpot
smiles in the Mediterranean light,
content in the world of huge simplicities.

Now I rejoice my very limbs, and risk
the grand gesture, a vague benediction,
yet pause at what my raised hand declares.
For how can I, naive, say what I affirm
unless I invent a new name for a blessing?

LIZARD

A blurred grey streak and he is gone
too fast for the eye to understand.
His track rustles dead stalks, makes
the leaves to shudder; then silence
over the mound of pebbles. And silently
he is there again on the white wall.

A tooled leather sheath
on miniature crocodile legs;
a fleck of granite eye
held by the saucer's rim;
each fluted foot
pointing in five directions;
a statuette of dust. Only
the jugular flutter shows
he has run a dark age,
stopped instantly, and holds
immobile in the glare.

Perfect heraldic emblem of day,
yet traveller from primaeval time;
the messenger of tombs transposed
to a stillness in sunlight.

Then the ancient head lifts slightly
in a decision. The wall is bare.

LION-TAMER

These days the crowds are thinner,
take holidays abroad and dislike circus fables.
Adults with glazed faces are tugged by children's shouts.

To weak applause the tamer steps in,
accoutrements complete — flat braid scribbled
across the chest, black leather hat, a sinuous whip.

Elegant, he strides his sahara
of the Big Top, fêted with the smell of hot sand
like a conqueror of deserts, one who manipulates the hour

with a frown and a gesture.
And indeed the beast begin to run
just as he intends. His voice lashes; hey, Rajah; up, Selim.

Reluctantly the circling lions
stop, and lock their clear and amber eyes
centrally upon him. No matter that they too are middle-aged

with fur balding in patches —
they too will serve, as will the man who leans
forward into their gaze. Together they set the tableau, explain

that what the arena holds
is always and only the stare of the encounter,
that, and as from a distance, the soft growl in the throat.

THE LION AND THE HAPPY VILLAGE

The drums of the village beat for three days
for the lion is dead.
The warrior chants of his spear, of how his arm
flashed like a cobra.
Now the villagers dance.

The farmer tells that his travelling soul has seen
that the lion is asleep.
His chin rests on his left paw, his hooks
twitch in their pads.
Now the villagers stand still.

The oldest man says he will sing of the dream
in the lion's head.
He is making pictures of brown and scarlet, he hears
the music of bones.
The villagers go home.

THE YELLOW BIRD AND THE POET

Lazy with sunlight, stretched under a tree

                    I happened to look up
To the lower branches. And there he was

            Yellow upon yellow and black
Like the soul of a butterfly become a finch.

            He nodded briskly at my stare,
His nimble eyes bright, mine brimming with praise.

            Then he crapped on my foot
And silently flew off, swooping down the valley.

SCENE WITH ANGLER

A sullen afternoon, the water dissolving
a thin grey light. The boat drifts
over aquatic memories, broadside to a lisping wind.

The loch spreads as wide as heaven
as complete with angels, who move
their occasional presence among its high deeps.

He peers into the ripple, eyes skimming
the corrugations of a sunken lifetime
for the slow rings that tell of an event.

A sedge sits praying on his left knee. He casts,
and casts, always to the half-remembered,
the misconstrued, his hunter's love denied,

sustained by recollection — how suddenly
his line flicked tight into a wide tangle of water
and his rod hummed to a revelation of silver.

GOING NORTH

Driving north, we fail to focus
the slipping line of the moors.
The shire drifts by,
brute distance for crossing, a green
of space to be eyed, not seen.

The road changes angle, and dips
to a new approach. Now we sense
the land begin to stir, to leap
to the present tense;
coming thunder puts weight into the air.

Once home rituals of the hearth
are celebrated, the blessings said.
We joke about the sleeping cat, make tea.
But what the fells were declaiming
stays in my head.

And I reproach myself for sloth.
Those dales were there for a hundred miles,
yet I saw no meaning
till chance did my work. Vision
should harvest more than a random gleaning.

NORTH FROM PENRITH

This land is irreversible.
It begins with tongue-shaped hills, yet
since these peaks first raised their heads
and turned their anguished faces into crags
no word has cracked the petrified silence.

A man and his dog climb the track to the steading;
for him too a landscape is what survives.
By the outcrop of the valley's ribs he goes
past the great stones strung like memories,
his eyes full of pebbles. Always for the man

whose past is behind him
all consequences have the quality of rock.

EXCLUDED BY MOUNTAINS

We have always believed in mountains,
their inwardness, and how they ascend
to perimeters of blue; high lords they are.

Their heads are always turned away,
their thoughts ruthless. Consider the essence
of stone, how men dying of thirst

will suck a pebble yet still go mad,
their senses unweighted. Reflect how the prophet
on finding truths as certain as flint

discovers them more obdurate than his own despair.
And how little the hand achieves on squeezing,
hard, even smallest grit, and bleeds on separation.

So do not expect, but extend your arm, touch
with most careful fingertips this huge rock,
and feel the cold surface of a great god's back.

STELLAR JOURNEY

Separate, though their bodies touch,
the spirits grope for a crack in the ceiling,
slip by the black and silver roofs,

gain the last cathedral spire
whitely angled above the river of ink
(his hand lying coiled on her abdomen)

up to tread the moon's domestic orbit;
thence distantly to Mars and the planetary stairs
to lighted plains, the floor of altitudes

where spiralled dust is an astral carpet
for mansions beyond — attenuation now a gas so rare
that meteorites may sail unwinking;

yet still the metaphysical hunger spreads
from the sleeping forms, who in their mating moment
sought only to find
a compact actuality.

2

A SHORT HISTORY OF GREEK STATUARY

It began with noises from treetrunks,
a muffled grumbling of gods and heroes
annoyed at long imprisonment in wood.
So craftsmen kindly let them out.

They stood at stiff attention, befitting
such a formal occasion. But the constraints
were out of character, for everyone knows
god never exchange a level stare

and have not heroes earned the right
to flex a biceps? So neck and elbow turned,
a knee advanced to swell the chiton.
And so they held, the god-men, a harmony

stretched taut as a well-strung lyre.
Yet still complaints continued. That hero,
Hercules no doubt, had a hernia in life
and wished his personality preserved;

the swing of that nymph's hips had caused
vast consequence, and merited remark.
So the statues were freed, and waived
and danced their way in blowsy liberty.

Meanwhile, the gods returned to the woods.

WITCH DAY

A bright day for burning. Peddlers sell
paper dolls; townsfolk idle in booths killing time
till the noon bell.

She's one who stared into coals, spoke
with the salamanders, copulated with spirits
that work in the smoke.

She who for heat bartered all our gain —
the small freedom from the demon's power,
the space in our pain.

That woman betrayed us, sought
through her sleights the primitive fusion
of flame and thought.

Which is unlawful. Good people, rest,
for now is the treason safely contained,
trapped in female flesh.

Let torch and priest advance five paces,
congregation step back from the rustling pyre,
hands held before faces
to shield them from the opening fire.

THE LINEAGE OF FAIR WOMEN

No, not a song to shrine your beauty
for who thinks now of Laura's gaze
or pictures how Beatrice stood? We grant
to much-sung women, by a lazy courtesy,
a satin couch in limbo, and cherish instead
the artifice of oaths by their marvelling dead.

So, I'll not describe: let me now
deny the lyric tug and flatly affirm
that sunlight never did better office
than in tracing the curve of your brow,
that clearest in all nature does your voice raise
within my ear leaping octaves of praise.

The timeless is unfashionable: your grace
displays a salvation we dare no longer seek,
shows to chaos the pattern of order
in the symmetry and circle of your face.
These are the seals, which are the warranty
of that famed lineage, by evidence of harmony.

This needs no swearing, for the actual you
is proof, and more than words my hand shall be
your faultless troubadour, knowing only what is true.

DRESS PARADE

They were recruited in a distant country
      nearly a lifetime ago
      though daily it grows clearer.
Mostly they scout alone, but today the company

has mustered, kitted in regulation style
      of patterned frock, large bag,
      hair bobbed neatly to a white helmet
and about the face the fluttering, apologetic smile

essential for such ceremonies. All have applied
      approximate lipstick, powder;
      now, in the undoubted scent of bathsalts
they sit fluting birdtalk — who was born, how he died.

So, over a teacup rim eyes hint conspiracy.
      Intelligence circulates
      discreet as a saucer's clink
as each inclines her head to murmur her latest victory,

tells how she slaughtered a certain day,
      left the hours dismembered
      and time, the enemy, compelled
again to go and wait, yield the right of way.

None here will ever refer to ultimate defeat.
      Instead the party ends
      with fingers clasped, laughter, advice
to wrap up warmly as they move to enfilade the street.

Later, along the frontiers of night, they mount
      to sentry duty,
      lay straight in their widowed beds
or in stiff, maiden sheets, stare at the dark, and count.

VICTORIAN SAMPLER

A perfect square of gilt, in which is described
a symmetry of peacock tails and floral curls
charged within a circle. Neutral as a lens
the glass shows both the scene and a way of seeing
— all objects as formality, motion in a pose.

Within this focussed eye for years
a woman sat; here is Time's counterpoint
secured in tiny stitches. That labour
makes her presence real, liberates her
to flutter about her duties, earnestly
exploring the light of her major meanings.

Such fantasies only confuse, for what is sure
is that her interludes passed in pondering
greys and greens and gold brocade. Other truths
have failed, save that now she weighs less
that the dead Victorian moth, like paper,
we recently found under the baize.

To be her life and decorate her missing name
now only these calm, inessential hours remain.

ENCOUNTER

A pretty girl, illuminated by her youth,
sits opposite. Such accidents occur
without regard for age-old mysteries
and half a lifetime leaping around,
circling their truth.

A finger of light touches her cheeks:
the down glistens. Gold is spun
from such enchantments, hair and skin
briefly transfigured emblazon
the icons we seek,

or once have sought. Now a sceptical eye
peers at those silky curves, and disbelieves:
no transcendental secrets there. But recall
how once an innocent god
stretched from the sky

to fashion such omens, who from a place
of perfect possibilities shook out
his gilded blessings on skin and hair,
and spread his magician's cloak, stitched
with stars in their race.

All long ago? This time knows
no dance upon the sacred ground,
builds nothing from the reasons why
heads gladly turn to admire her legs
as she rises, goes.

TWO OF YOU

You both sit in that chair.
After so very long an absence
     I stare
at a face grown rounder, colour
     of hair
too carefully preserved. Places
you mention are remote,
     sound bare.

You lean back, and instantly
there's the other you, arrived
     unmistakably —
that arc of a smile, the young wrist
     on your knee.
The known eyes light; sometimes
we laugh on the moment, quite
     familiarly.

This pairing, the flickering view
dances on, for alone neither person
     holds true;
two actors distinct on the stage
     where you
are the plot, and who hinting
your story must pace out
     mine too.

BONFIRE IN APRIL

No emblem, this; not a ducal banner
Of pluming clouds, no circlet of gold to crown
A lord of autumn in his scarlet and brown,
Just a fire to clear junk in the laziest manner.

Old prunings with their fingers now gone brittle,
A tangle of couchgrass still sprouting in force,
Plastic bags, even half a headless wooden horse
From storybook summers when the children were little.

It must have been me who hoed round this spot,
Played father, was a man who had reasons
For inhabiting a place and marking the seasons.
Tried to raise a few plants, tossed others to rot.

Perhaps after all those flowers really mattered —
The fuschia's hats for elves, hydrangea's lace —
Which a basic husbandry brought to this space.
Their dance is lost now, their finery scattered.

I add another forkload to the pile, stoke
The spitting grey pyramid's one wispy flame
And squint through smarting eyelids to reclaim
The shape of the years in the acrid smoke.

WELCOME, LAD

Look at this, they said.
So for a moment you stared, puzzled
at this distraction
from childhood plans, till your eyes escaped
with a truant giggle.

Now practice this, they said.
Sometimes you obliged and were snared,
or sometimes measured
a simple wile against their strongarm
before being overcome.

Naturally you had no weapons,
yet till near the end you defended exits,
hedged a space
where small strengths could revel and run
in miniature freedom.

Stand in line, they said,
perturbed by your sapling height. My, my,
you're taller than your father
who abetted those men, even while blessing
all they drove away.

Growth is partly subtraction,
a loss of former grace. Always they carved
and commanded and pressed
as yearly the bones were shaped, and your posture
grew to their final angle.

Now step up, I say,
my love dumb and glad; see, I salute
your newly-finished smile;
come and join the men;
welcome, lad, to your disinheritance.

WITH MY SISTER

It was cold enough that day to cloud your eyes
    with a bitter ice on the air
piercing as death, and with a sky as hard
as the ground which awaited the three of us there.

Afterwards, indoors, we were still too raw to talk
    and had no reason for trying;
the fact was always in nature and half accepted.
I did not grieve the simple event of his dying.

Rather it was the exile, the breaking of a man
    now barred from his private space,
his secrets to be filched or buried, his warmth dispersed,
how all he'd assembled would drift out of place.

I wept for the going of all the loved particulars
    whose order set his life.
Yet we hurried his ending when, like accomplices,
we sat and deliberately took as keepsakes
for you his ring, to me the silver penknife.

3

THE BALLAD OF GENTLE JOHN
(In memory of M.C.)

Gentle John had fists of iron,
and twenty victories to his credit,
yet a clear eye and an unscarred brow;
one of the strong, who shall not inherit.

John rarely used his limbs of steel
(equating violence with shame).
From a rather different talent
grew the flower of his local fame —

he had the gift of sitting still
and a sweet capacity to listen.
Weaker men sniffed out his strength,
wheeled like a flock, their eyes aglisten,

and with ageing dames and worried youths
came for their therapeutic hour
to the Rose and Crown, their faltering souls
to charge with John's quiet power.

Cousin Fred and Neighbour Sam
played lieutenants to that troop,
and John would hear them, looking composed,
not letting his massive shoulders droop.

O a nod it has a healing charm,
and words serve less than a courteous ear.
So John sat, head slightly bent,
gazing firmly into his beer.

Home early one day John entered his house
and paused in the sitting-room door;
Wife Nancy and a travelling man
were a naked starfish on the floor.

John left in silence, walked down the street
and out to the utmost edge of town,
went into a field to sit on a rock,
puzzled the clouds did not fall down.

He thought of a drink with Neighbour Sam
or an hour with his Cousin Fred.
He rose from his place, returned to the house,
and went and hanged himself instead.

THE BOND

Angry eyes burn at the paper.
The evidence is somewhere here
of what you said. Remember? You signed your name.

The lawyer had daffodils on his desk.
A fidgeting nib scratched parchment;
the mantelpiece clock, an ebony cyclops,
dilated its wide and benevolent gaze.
Contingencies paced quietly in the shadows.

So many clauses, like a basket
to hold the air; signatures black as dried blood;
the seal a wax confection. There was a contract,

yes, most certainly, for once by the estuary
the couple, arm in arm, came to a rockface
towering high in the tidal wind, its battlements
inviolable amd ordering all the circling land.
Every intention led only to that moment.

There was a party of the first part,
now older, more confused. Voices are raised.
It was all set down — who you said you were

and where you were going, the price
to be paid with tedium and laughter,
and the time to run till the end of days.

Now eyes squint through the wisps of smoke
to the clean white page where once were words.

THE HOMECOMING

There were great birds circling.
Clearly the portents were all awry, the hour perturbed.
From the city breathless messengers began to arrive,
choking with news, and the shouting drew nearer.

But his wife sat with her maid, in tranquillity,
even when the shrubs were trampled down
by the hubbub of neighbours.

Lazarus stood in the doorway, staring, reading her
in silence. Uneasy, he drifted to the table
prepared elaborately against his homecoming,
but the bread had only the known taste of death.

Why had he returned? Once his beloved has deeply grieved,
and revived, and lifted her head to breathe again
— such a man stays dead forever.

A WIFE DESERTED

The house is silent, still full of departure.
Blinking, she climbs the stair
and gasps in the empty air,
tries not to inhale the scent of absence.

In time anaesthetic white will replace
the tracks of easy tears,
will politely cover her fears
with a cicatrized, lopsided mask.

But meanwhile she grieves walleyed
as the blind might mourn,
for all her meanings have been torn,
her mysteries point nowhere.

THE MAZE

They understood each other well.
Up there the sungod in his golden rooms,
and below, brutality prowling the sewers.

So many seekers! Not only the Athenian boy
with his ribbon, who stabbed so earnestly
and boasted a rare return to light,

but all the others who must hunt down corridors
for the ceaseless bellow of anguish, stumbling
till they perish in their maze.

The beast? A twitching, massive, horned head
swivelling murderously, with blood on cheek
or faceless, as your history decides.

He shambles close, yet so nearly invisible,
the eyes glowing black in the hot dark, that men
speak of the labyrinth called Minotaur.

And who may tell the heart of the matter?
Perhaps there is always a central, legendary dread,
and round it, corner pointing to corner,
the unfinished web of loss, the catacombs of pain.

REFLECTIONS IN A TROJAN POOL

1
The quay brimming with baskets,
great circles clustered tightly
to make squares of willow.
And the gaping fish, their rainbow scales
lit like small flames
in the white sunlight.

An army of masts creak in the bay,
and the painted eyes of boats
gaze obliquely at the jetty wall.
Short, olive men lounge in the bowsprites,
applaud two Negro boys
wrestling between the coils of rope.

Pause, voice. The dust hangs still in Mycenae.
Shadows of cypresses stripe the silent road
to the port, where today no ship
departs or homes. Yet Agamemnon's wealth is here,
these men, these vessels
are his morning thoughts.

And the heat and the rotting smell grow murderous
between the enamelled blue of sky and the flat sea
dazzling over the straits to Troy.

2
Troy, dirty as any other harbour.
Square Phoenician sails, now furled.
The wine tastes like rust, and the whores
daub green and blue on their eyelids.

Linger, voice, in the telling.

Behind, on a hunchback hill
the acropolis — earthworks topped
with boulders to protect the cisterns
and the archers among the oiljars.

And from these rocks we now invent

the gleaming battlements of Troy,
marble rising massively, sheer
to the banners fluttering like kites
in the clean Aegean air.

Linger in the telling of it.

3
In these northern latitudes
the light is lost and grey,
the city built of winter dusk.

Winds keen past granite,
and sometimes drive the rain
obliquely as falling arrows.

Yet who leans over water
may see himself reflected
flickering in a Trojan pool.

4
Europe's imagination begins with disaster:
for Troy has fallen, and for all time.

Though six more towns may rise yet Troy is broken:
no resurrection cancels a real death.

Though endlessly the sea laves the beaches
the mark endures, and the authentic city haunts us

by so intense an absence. And as the city
so the man, each with his eyes aslant,

for neither rocks nor walls in dreams
can keep the citadel that keeps his pride.

Young people of my northern shores, put on
your blues and gay white, go walking

past the ships, the quays. But stop your ears
to the waves, and be deaf to the telling of it:

avoid all reflections in a Trojan pool.

POEM IN THE MIRROR

The irony of personal loss
blots out a universe of pain.

Hold to such an hour. It is
the mirror of the naked soul

revealing bone and hunger unadorned
behind whatever face a man might proffer.

And as the world ticks again into motion,
mechanical, steel-grey before the shoots

of the new and acid Spring emerge,
hold yet within the ear

the cry of the wolf baying in winter
for all he has lost, and cannot find.

AN ERROR

So summer isn't over, after all?
Those misty days deceived; the bounding sun
Just stumbled briefly but didn't fall.

And what of that friend we buried last week?
He claimed he was dead, had left the usual mess
Not having brought his garden to its peak

Nor set his house and wife in order.
He too was in error, and grinning must mend
His wrongful trespass over death's border.

He will not find his days more slack, nor nights
More desperate than before we covered his face,
But having once departed and cancelled these streets
Bewildered will grope towards his usual place.

Here comes that puzzled dead man, who speaks, who writes.

MONOLOGUE WITH TULIP

I have you fixed, young androgyne.
Tulifa vulgans. There, I name you
and so control your parts, which means
possession. For years I have sighted you
easily triangulated in a corner bed,
sniffed your odourless presence, known
the condescension of your leaves
to the rattling wind. I could sketch
your xylem caverns, list your moods by colours,
deliver your history from Holland's memory.
All ways I grasp you, however meekly
you stand on your woman's waist
raising two cupped hands
to chalice air in a volume of yellow.

I know too that you escape me
disappearing through a shy, sly miracle
of metamorphosis into yourself.
Secretive, you turn your tulip back
as always, Love, when the familiar
moves away to its own impersonal place.
Now fully clothed, answering no name
nor trapped by any symbol
you challenge me once more
by your proper strangeness, that green
of jungles, yellow rare as goblin's gold.
Therefore I start your recapture
plucking your instances by armfuls
to gather your whispers, to bring you home.

4

ST. CHRYSTOBOLE

"Thy fires, Lord, which blazing rim
the fierce horizon of the world.
Thy nails of pain extend each limb,
define the human form, teaching us
open-armed embrace of Your loss."

St. Chrystobole rose from bleeding knee,
took up his book and from the wall
a wooden cross to goad his journey,
went to seek out unending pain
to learn to celebrate its name.

He chose to dwell among cactus blades
by the rocks at the tawny desert's edge.
Through the years he every moment prayed,
eyes tightly shut in a wilderness
of sand and grief and his distress.

But slowly, in that nameless place,
the ache grew less compelling;
as one who construes a familiar face
attention flickered, and what he sought
would slip aside in a drifting thought.

Heat bent his head and stilled his psalm.
The desert mice observed wide-eyed
how against the stump of a withered palm
St. Chrystobole, that godly one,
sat dozing in the evening sun.

KEEPER OF THE HOUSE

The house he loyally served was grey and tall,
with windows massively barred.
Inside all was iron, the cells rising in galleries
from a grilled entrance hall.

Each evening he walked the corridors, attended
his sad duties, ticked the roll —
Cowardice, Lechery, Fraud — the names flowed easily
though the faces blended.

With each he sat down to reminisce a while,
enjoyed the story again, shared
their laughter in the pleasure and sweep of it,
moved on with a smile.

All doors locked, after the last cordial parting
he descended to his chair
for the final task. Grieving with guilt he sat,
head sunk low, and the tears starting.

OCTOBER CITY

Through the autumn drizzle,
streetlamps are pearls,
longlooped above the shine of damp pavements.

In the houses dissolving
in dusk, yellow windows
form arpeggios. Almost I am convinced

by philosophies of bright and dark.

For the city redeems itself
in chiaroscuro, mass;
even in the shade of plane trees

the railings gleam
as in an old etching
and balancing the black, pull the world to rights.

Almost I am convinced
but pause at the argument
of the muffled men on the bombsite

their circles of faces
over outstretched hands
at a small fire that spits against the wet.

Such a harmony of light, such a cold despair.

HERMIT

The private man within his skin
defines a universe, hermetically enclosing
an earth and firmament within.
Meteors fleck the space
behind the curtains of his face.

Within that void his sight may ride
a lonely distance to infinitude.
Yet turning his head to one side
brings his gaze to mesh
in the tangles of his flesh.

And guests will visit, who whimsically wear
a clown's red nose, or come dressed
in drama of mourning to signal despair.
Such figures make his memory,
people his ghost society.

Thus the private man in his private hour,
who sometimes weeps like a flailing infant
threshing his arms in a waste of power
until the pain
is reconciled, and part of the vision again.

LATE REHEARSAL

The theatre of insomnia
is only for rehearsals,
most often after the play has ended
— for that was merely one account, and the audience
still waits in the familiar dark.

A spotlight brightens.
Figures begin to circle
pacing the stage just so, and on cue
precisely select, though with no freedom, those words
that might fix a history in time.

Pause, and begin again.
Once more the hunters
stalk the clues to a perfect tragedy.
Yet truths will not be spellbound into place;
this version too must be deleted.

But how these actors
would falter, perplexed,
at how with no concern for memories
a child or Spring will skip in the open air
with such a beautiful lack of caution.

THERAPIST

The shadow of a leaf falls upon the page
and as the breeze moves the shape skitters
    as if writing my notes.
    Yes I am listening, really,
although what I hear matters much less
than what you say. You were supposing
    that you might be human
    complete with genitals, greed
and enough cowardice to survive a day —
just an example, not specially wrong.
    I agree (with this and more).
    Yet you imply your history
requires a unique and loving repair.
I think that where you have come from
    depends on where you are now,
    but together we'll make a fable;
it seems we can manage a doubtful future
    provided we have a past.

Now you falter. Here we should attend
more closely. For though I am slowly learning
    those things of which
    it is better to be silent
for you perhaps the ache is too raw;
we'll honour your reticence, yet mark the place.
    There is time, oh indeed
    time will be your rack.
In the new quiet you gaze at me directly
and I half-expect you to surprise me, saying
    how you find in the end
    the personal is not enough.
I return your stare, and together we listen
to the gathering wind in the boughs outside.

WHITE GLADIOLI

A week of work unfinished
and our guests arriving soon. All day
you have been as tense as a swarm of bees.
Your urgency shuts me out.

Briskly you angle the gladioli
into the waiting vase. Perhaps they are
my messengers, to detain you into hearing
what the hour does not admit —

how white may curl, light green thrust high,
the necessity of stillness.

IT IS NOT VIVALDI

The record ends, clicks, slows to be still.
Standing alone by the window I realise
that in fortunate moments what perplexes
is not Vivaldi but the mundane world.
Here the conviction of his perfect discourse
hangs in the air of the awe-filled room,
yet outside the panes the breeze
takes nothing to the glowering fields
and the hills stand off, guarding their silence.
In the suburbs the corners of houses
point nowhere, and traffic groans
in a modulation of changing gears
to destinations in improbable places.
True, there are lines of pink in the dusk
and slips of light will chink through curtains
but beauty alone is not the question.

Climbing the stairs in a fortunate moment
I meet you hurrying from the shower,
your skin thinking only of warm towels.
There is your usual body, familiar
in a hundred moods and no longer glamorous
despite the red in your hair.
But still your surface bounds the space
Vivaldi lived in; so too
the pearls of water run like notes
in the cadences which made his thought.
I have studied long to know this music.
Say, what discipline could yield
with equal clarity the sight and smell
of soil, the stones, the stupid wind?

WALKING TOGETHER AT LYNE POOL IN WINTER

After days
With arched and naked trees
Flailing the side of the storm,
New sunlight,
And the season ignites
A brittle, sparkling harvest.

Along the road
Diagonal white shadows
Inch back, and frost retreats
With the same line.
Such fine exactitude disturbs
The comfort of gloved senses.

The brilliants
Which crust the towpath ice
Rivet themselves to the retina.
May the eye
Manufactured so truly
Retain its clean seeing.

A copse
Of birch at the water's edge,
Still etched in rime,
Creaks and drips.
Revived, the ageless river runs
Collecting reversed appearances.

Now cuts the frozen lanscape, sharp
As a pointed diamond.
Essences
Stand clear in solitude.
No man can live this way.

Treacherous walking.
But these encounters with desolation
Reclaimed and turned in light
May best survive
Fading afternoon, with so much uncertain
In the coming dark,
Your human hand gone.

QUESTION FOR A QUIET EVENING

Since poems are prayers which are never answered
    what do they hope to gain
who make a church of language?
Poetry will not mend our morals
or even pay the rent; your hand
will sleep as loosely in mine
    whatever the verse may pretend.

Perhaps they are hoping for a celebration
    as when bells ring out
lending their own bright honour
to the bare calendar. Words certainly
should dance at every festival, as now
when your profile turns in the light
and a moment becomes an occasion.

Or perhaps they aspire to a perfect order
    as in a country house
where room-high tapestry displays
how smiling men win a battle
while immobile birds hover forever.
Sufficient, then, to be a stitch
    in such a precisely balanced kingdom.

But mostly I think that the wish is to say
    what absolutely cannot be said.
And I glance at the shadows on the wall
as we linger in the kitchen over coffee
using the language of settled affection,
shadows which mock and never relent
    but, briefly, may be placated.